2004 | General

[BLANK PAGE]

FOR OFFICIAL USE

G

KU   PS

Total Marks

0560/402

NATIONAL
QUALIFICATIONS
2004

THURSDAY, 13 MAY
10.20 AM – 11.35 AM

COMPUTING STUDIES
STANDARD GRADE
General Level

Fill in these boxes and read what is printed below.

Full name of centre

Town

Forename(s)

Surname

Date of birth

Day Month Year   Scottish candidate number   Number of seat

Read each question carefully.

Attempt **all** questions.

Write your answers in the space provided on the question paper.

Write as neatly as possible.

Answer in sentences wherever possible.

Before leaving the examination room you must give this book to the invigilator. If you do not, you may lose all the marks for this paper.

SCOTTISH
QUALIFICATIONS
AUTHORITY

SAB 0560/402 6/27220

©

1. Kraivie High School would like a poster for pupils telling them about their Activity Day.

First draft

KHS Activity Day

Learning can be fun
Make new friends
Learn a new skill

The first draft looked too plain so a second draft was created.

Second draft

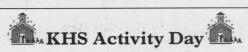 **KHS Activity Day**

Learning can be fun
Make new friends
Learn a new skill

(*a*) State **two** changes that have been made to the **heading text** in the second draft.

1 _____

2 _____

2
1
0

(*b*) (i) The picture of the school has been scaled. What does the term *scale* mean?

_____

_____

1
0

(ii) State **two** other changes which have been made to the graphic.

_____

_____

_____

2
1
0

1. **(continued)**

(*c*) The school wishes to put a photograph of pupils on the poster.

Which input device would be needed?

_____

1
0

(*d*) The school has a black and white *laser printer* and a number of *ink jet printers*.

(i) Give **one** advantage of using the laser printer.

_____

_____

1
0

(ii) Give **one** disadvantage of using the laser printer.

_____

_____

1
0

(*e*) One of the teachers said that the *running costs* of the ink jet printer were high.

Give an example of a running cost.

_____

1
0

(*f*) The poster was created using a *program file* and a *datafile*.

(i) Explain the term "program file".

_____

_____

1
0

(ii) Explain the term "datafile".

_____

_____

1
0

[Turn over

2. Kraivie High School sends out individual letters to parents giving details of the activities their child has chosen. On reading through the letter, it is noticed that instead of "Activity Day" the words "Activity Week" have been printed throughout the document.

(*a*) What feature of the word processing software would allow this mistake to be easily corrected in one operation?

_____

(*b*) The school used *standard paragraphs* to create these letters. Explain the term "standard paragraph".

_____

_____

(*c*) When the completed letter was printed it did not fit onto one page. Name **two** changes which would allow the letter to fit onto one page.

1 _____

_____

2 _____

_____

(*d*) A pupil at the school suggested to the school secretary that she make use of the *on-line tutorial* feature of the package.

Explain the term "on-line tutorial".

_____

_____

_____

2. (continued)

(e) The school used an integrated package to create the letter.

Give **two** benefits to the user of using an integrated package.

1 _____

_____

2 _____

_____

(f) The school computers operate a *WIMP* style of *HCI*.

(i) What do the letters "HCI" stand for?

H _____ C _____ I _____

(ii) Why might users like using the WIMP style of HCI?

_____

_____

(g) A reporter calls at the school to write an article about the Activity Day. He uses a *palmtop computer* to make notes.

(i) Why would the reporter find a palmtop computer useful for this task?

_____

_____

(ii) The palmtop computer uses an *LCD* screen.

What do the letters "LCD" stand for?

L _____ C _____ D _____

(iii) A special pen is used instead of a keyboard to input data.

What is the name given to this data input method?

H _____ R _____

[Turn over

KU	PS

3. Kraivie High School has decided to use the school's computer system to help manage and run the Activity Day Program.

A *datafile* containing some of the details of the Activity Day is shown below.

Forename	Surname	Sex	Year	Event	Transport
Jade	Forbes	F	2	Photography	No
Gavin	Ross	M	1	Football	Yes
Franki	Murphy	F	1	Golf	No
Barry	Miller	M	3	Cinema	Yes
Kiran	Ahmed	F	2	Skating	Yes

(a) The datafile has to be changed to include the cost for each event.

Explain how this could be done.

_____

_____

_____

2 1 0

(b) (i) A list of all activities which need transport is required.

Describe how you could use the database package to obtain this information.

_____

_____

2 1 0

(ii) The list of activities is needed in alphabetic order.

Describe how this could be achieved.

_____

_____

2 1 0

(c) The computers in the school are linked together to form a *local-area network* (LAN).

Give **two** advantages, to the user, of using a LAN.

1 _____

_____

2 _____

_____

2 1 0

KU	PS

3. **(continued)**

(*d*) The teachers are concerned that pupils may try to access the Activity Day datafile and alter the activities on offer.

State **two** ways this could be prevented.

1 _____

_____

2 _____

_____

(*e*) All the network users have the choice of saving to a *floppy disk* or a *hard disk* on the network.

(i) Give **one** advantage of saving to floppy disk.

_____

_____

(ii) Give **one** advantage of saving to the hard disk on the network.

_____

_____

[Turn over

4. Kraivie High School has decided to use a spreadsheet to keep track of the Activity Day finances.

The spreadsheet is shown below.

	A	B	C	D	E	F
1	Activity	No of children	Cost per child	Pupils to pay	School to pay	Total Cost to school
2	Cinema	80	6	4.5	1.5	£120.00
3	Football	60	1.5	1	0.5	£30.00
4	Golf	30	3.5	3	0.5	£15.00
5	Photography	20	2.25	2	0.25	£5.00
6	Skating	100	6	4.5	1.5	£150.00
7					TOTAL	£320.00

(a) Some figures are calculated automatically by the use of *formulae*.

  (i) In which cells would each formula appear?

    =B3*E3   would appear in cell _____

    =C3–D3   would appear in cell _____

  (ii) State the formula which would appear in cell F7 _____

(b) A new event of Web Design is to be entered on the spreadsheet.

State the changes which will have to be made to include this activity in the correct place.

_____

_____

_____

(c) Columns C, D and E should have been displayed as money.

Describe the steps needed to make these changes.

1 _____

2 _____

Page eight

4. (continued)

(*d*) In column A the word "photography" does not fit properly into the cell. How would you solve this problem?

_____

_____

[Turn over

KU	PS
	1
	0

5. Kraivie High School has an account at Cheapest Ever Cash and Carry. The store is visited before Activity Day to purchase snacks for the pupils.

(a) Here is the school's account number   000136164749

(i) Which digit is the check digit?

_____

(ii) What is the purpose of a check digit?

_____

_____

(iii) How is a check digit created?

_____

_____

(b) The shopping can be paid for by cash or *Electronic Funds Transfer* (EFT).

(i) Give **one** advantage to the shopper of paying by EFT.

_____

_____

(ii) Give **one** advantage to the store of the customers using EFT.

_____

_____

(c) The shop assistants key in sales details at a *terminal*.

Explain the term "terminal".

_____

5. **(continued)**

(*d*) The store stock records are updated at the end of each working day. This is an example of *batch processing*.

Give **two** advantages to the store of using batch processing.

1 _____

_____

2 _____

_____

(*e*) A *transaction file* is used to update the *master file*.

(i) What is a "transaction file"?

_____

_____

(ii) Give an example of data which may be held in the store's transaction file.

_____

_____

(*f*) The manager of the store has introduced a *voice recognition system* to restrict access to the main office.

Give **one** advantage and **one** disadvantage to the store of introducing this system.

Advantage

_____

Disadvantage

_____

[Turn over

6. At the skating rink on Kraivie High School's Activity Day, the pupils watched the Automated Rink Sweeper travel at speed round the rink, cleaning the ice.

(*a*) Give **two** safety precautions that could be taken to ensure that no skater was hit by the Sweeper.

1 _____

2 _____

(*b*) (i) The Sweeper uses *real-time processing*.

Explain the term "real-time".

_____

_____

(ii) Name another type of processing.

_____

(*c*) The Sweeper has been programmed using a *high level language*.

(i) Give **two** advantages of using a high level language.

1 _____

_____

2 _____

_____

(ii) Part of the ice rink has to be blocked off and the Sweeper will not be allowed to access this area.

What will have to be done to the **computer** controlling the Sweeper?

_____

6. **(continued)**

(d)   (i)   The Sweeper's *sensors* send *feedback* to the computer.

Explain the following terms.

Sensor _____

_____

Feedback _____

_____

(ii)   Is the Sweeper an example of an *open loop* system or a *closed loop* system?

_____

(e)   The computer controlling the Sweeper is running under an *operating system*.

State **two** tasks an operating system would carry out.

1 _____

2 _____

(f)   Give **two** advantages to the management of using an Automated Sweeper.

1 _____

_____

2 _____

_____

[*END OF QUESTION PAPER*]

[BLANK PAGE]

[BLANK PAGE]

C

0560/403

NATIONAL QUALIFICATIONS 2004	THURSDAY, 13 MAY 1.00 PM – 2.45 PM	**COMPUTING STUDIES STANDARD GRADE** Credit Level

Read each question carefully.

Attempt **all** questions.

Write your answers in the answer book provided. **Do not** write on the question paper.

Write as neatly as possible.

Answer in sentences wherever possible.

SCOTTISH
QUALIFICATIONS
AUTHORITY

SAB   0560/403   6/18520   ©

	KU	PS

1. Iona is a secretary for a software development company. She sends out many *standard letters* to customers.

(*a*)   (i) What is a standard letter? — KU **2**

     (ii) What is the name of the process in which information from a *datafile* is inserted into the standard letter? — KU **1**

(*b*) A record from the customer datafile is shown below.

Field Name	Sample Data	Field Size
Name	Chang, Alistair	40
Address	26, Station Road	80
Town	Westbury	20
Postcode	WY34 2NH	8
Age	24	2

   (i) How much memory does a single record from the database need? — PS **1**

   (ii) How many records from the database could you fit onto a floppy disk that holds 1·44 Mb? — PS **3**

(*c*)   (i) Name the legislation that protects the rights of the customers whose details are held in the database. — KU **1**

     (ii) Describe **two** rights that this legislation gives the customers. — KU **2**

(*d*) Before printing the letters, Iona always *spell checks* them. Describe in detail how a spell checker works. — KU **2**

(*e*) Name the piece of software that is required to ensure that the printout is the same as it appears on screen. — KU **1**

	KU	PS

2. Many buildings have air conditioning systems installed to control the temperature. The system warms up or cools down the building as necessary using heaters and fans.

(a) (i) What device is required to provide *feedback* of the temperature to the system? **1**

    (ii) Is this system an example of an *open loop* or *closed loop* system? **1**

    (iii) What type of processing is required for this system? **1**

    (iv) The temperature can vary continuously. What must be done to the temperature readings so that they are in a form that the computer can process? **1**

(b) The software used to control this system is held on a *ROM chip*.

    (i) Give **two** advantages of holding the software on a ROM chip. **2**

    (ii) Give **one** disadvantage of holding the software on a ROM chip. **1**

(c) The software is written using a *control language*. Give **one** reason why this is the most suitable language. **1**

(d) Give **one** advantage of using a computerised system rather than a manual system. **1**

[Turn over

	KU	PS

3. Tanya uses a spreadsheet to keep track of her fantasy football team. A section of the spreadsheet is shown below.

	A	B	C	D	E	F
1	Position	Player ID	Player Name	Player Cost (£m)	Week 1 Score	Week 2 Score
2	Goalkeeper	113	J Davidson	3.3	−2	1
3	Defender	202	H Hart	4.4	6	2
4	Defender	209	F Janario	4.1	6	2
5	Defender	273	J McTavish	3.0	0	9
6	Defender	298	B Parnevik	2.8	1	4
7	Midfielder	407	F Leconte	5.1	3	3
8	Midfielder	445	M Daniel	4.7	1	0
9	Midfielder	501	C Michaels	4.5	6	0
10	Forward	601	H Thierry	8.0	7	3
11	Forward	621	J Foe	5.6	3	2
12	Forward	247	D Christian	4.4	6	6
13						
14			TOTALS	49.9	37	32
15	Funds available (£m)	50				
16	Valid team?	YES				

(a) Formulae are used to calculate the column totals in cells **D14**, **E14** and **F14**. The formula in cell **D14** was *replicated* into the other two cells.

   (i) What is meant by the term "replicate"?

1

   (ii) When the formula was replicated, was *relative referencing* or *absolute referencing* used? Explain your answer.

2

(b) Cell **B16** contains a formula to show if a team is valid or not. A team is valid if the total player cost in **D14** is less than or equal to the funds available in **B15**. If a team is valid, the cell shows "YES" and if not, the cell shows "NO". Part of the formula used is given below. What should be entered into the spaces marked A and B?

$$= \underline{\quad} \; (\underline{\quad} , \text{"YES"}, \text{"NO"})$$

     ↑   ↑

     A   B

2

	KU	PS

3. (continued)

(*c*) Tanya uses the chart feature of her spreadsheet software to display her weekly scores. When data is added to the spreadsheet, the chart is updated automatically. What type of *data linkage* is this?

1

(*d*) Competitors in the fantasy league have the choice of registering their fantasy team by post or on the league's website.

   (i) Name **one** piece of computer hardware and **one** piece of software that Tanya requires to make use of the Internet.

2

  (ii) The Internet site is *multi-access*. What is meant by this term?

2

 (iii) Give **two** reasons why Tanya prefers to use the Internet rather than the post to register her team.

2

[Turn over

	KU	PS

	KU	PS

4. Safeprice Superstores is a chain of supermarkets that have stores all over Scotland.

Each store has a central computer with a database that holds details on all of the products that it sells. An example of a record from the database is shown below.

Product ID	002315
Product Manufacturer	Gimballs
Product Name	Chicken Soup
Product Price	£0·57
Stock Level	246
Reorder Level	150
Reorder?	N
Total Value of Stock	£140·22

(a) When a product is purchased, the *barcode* on the product is scanned and the information on the barcode is used to locate the product in the database.

   (i) How is the reading of a barcode validated?   **KU 1**

   (ii) Which field in the database is **always** updated when a product has been purchased?   **PS 1**

   (iii) Should this database be stored on backing storage media with *random access* or *sequential access*? Give a reason for your answer.   **PS 2**

(b) The manager of the shop is going to reduce the price of all products manufactured by Gimballs that cost over £0·50. Describe how the database could be used to produce a list of all the products that will be reduced in price.   **PS 3**

(c) The "Total Value of Stock" field is a *computed field*. What is meant by the term "computed field"?   **KU 1**

(d) Many customers use *electronic funds transfer* at *point of sale* to pay for their shopping.

   (i) Describe the process of electronic funds transfer.   **KU 3**

   (ii) Give **one** reason why many customers prefer this method of payment.   **PS 1**

(e) The individual points of sale are *remote terminals*. From what are the terminals remote?   **KU 1**

	KU	PS

5. Rhona is a computer programmer who works for a company which writes software for schools. She programs using a *high level language*.

(*a*) Give **one** difference between a high level language and a low level language.

    KU **1**

(*b*) (i) When developing the software, what type of *translator* would you suggest that Rhona should use? Give a reason for your answer.

    PS **2**

    (ii) Name the translator which converts low level language to machine code.

    KU **1**

(*c*) Rhona always writes software that is *portable*.

    (i) What is meant by the term "portable"?

    KU **1**

    (ii) Why is making the software portable an advantage to the company?

    PS **1**

(*d*) How does the Copyright, Designs and Patents Act protect Rhona's work?

    PS **1**

(*e*) Rhona's programs are very valuable and she does not want to lose any of the work that she has done. What should she do to ensure that none of her software is lost?

    PS **2**

(*f*) Rhona tries to develop programs that are *user friendly*.

    (i) To make the software user friendly, should she make the software *command driven* or *menu driven*? Explain your answer.

    KU **2**

    (ii) State **two** other ways in which software can be made more user friendly.

    PS **2**

[Turn over for Question 6 on *Page eight*

	KU	PS

6. All computer systems consist of *input devices*, *output devices*, *backing storage devices* and the *central processing unit*.

   (*a*)   (i)   Which part of the central processing unit is responsible for running a program correctly? — **1**

   (ii)   Which part of the central processing unit carries out calculations and decision-making processes? — **1**

   (*b*)   There are different types of memory in a computer system.

   (i)   What type of memory holds the data and instructions while a program is running? — **1**

   (ii)   What type of memory holds programs that never change? — **1**

   (*c*)   One task of the processor is *resource allocation*. Describe this task. — **2**

   (*d*)   Some computer systems are not *multimedia*. Suggest **one** input device and **one** output device that would be added to a computer system to make it multimedia. — **2** (PS)

   (*e*)   (i)   When you buy a piece of software, it usually comes on a *CD-ROM*. Give **two** reasons why this medium may be more suitable for this task than using floppy disks. — **2** (PS)

   (ii)   The *operating system* is involved in loading software from the CD-ROM. Name a function of the operating system and describe how it is used in this situation. — **2** (PS)

[*END OF QUESTION PAPER*]

[BLANK PAGE]

FOR OFFICIAL USE

G

	KU	PS
Total Marks		

0560/402

NATIONAL
QUALIFICATIONS
2005

THURSDAY, 12 MAY
G/C 9.00 AM – 10.15 AM
F/**G** 10.20 AM – 11.35 AM

COMPUTING STUDIES
STANDARD GRADE
General Level

Fill in these boxes and read what is printed below.

Full name of centre

Town

Forename(s)

Surname

Date of birth

Day Month Year

Scottish candidate number

Number of seat

Read each question carefully.

Attempt **all** questions.

Write your answers in the space provided on the question paper.

Write as neatly as possible.

Answer in sentences wherever possible.

Before leaving the examination room you must give this book to the invigilator. If you do not, you may lose all the marks for this paper.

SCOTTISH
QUALIFICATIONS
AUTHORITY

SAB 0560/402 6/22270

©

1. Pupils in 1st and 2nd year of a secondary school are going on a team building weekend. The details are stored in a *database*. Below is an example of a *record*.

Name:	Natalya Corrieri
Year:	2nd
House:	Bardowie
Emergency contact:	01334 82566
Medical condition:	Asthma

(a) A parent wants to see the records of all pupils held on this database. Does he have the right to see **all** records?

_____

Explain your answer.

_____

_____

(b) Describe how the guidance teacher would be able to get a *hardcopy* of only those 1st year pupils who are in Bardowie House.

_____

_____

_____

_____

(c) A new pupil has joined the school in 2nd year.

What must be done to include his details in the file?

_____

_____

(d) How can the school prevent unauthorised access to the computerised pupil files?

_____

KU	PS

1. (continued)

(e) The database is held on the school *LAN*.

What do the initials "LAN" stand for?

_____

(f) Some teachers at the school do not know very much about computers. Fortunately the database uses a *Graphical User Interface*. Give **two** reasons why this type of interface is useful for beginners.

1 _____

_____

2 _____

_____

(g) A lot of printing has been done and the Guidance department has been asked to pay towards *running costs*. Give **two** running costs of having the records printed out.

1 _____

2 _____

(h) The guidance teacher makes a second copy which she stores on a floppy disk.

What is this second copy called?

_____

[Turn over

2. A letter is to be sent out to parents telling them what pupils must take on the team building weekend.

(a) In the letter the year head has been named **many times** as Mrs Smith, whereas it should be Mrs Smythe.

(i) Name the feature of a word processing package which is used to make this change.

_____

(ii) Describe how the feature is used in the above example.

_____

_____

_____

(b) The letter includes a *standard paragraph* used for all school trips.

What is a "standard paragraph"?

_____

_____

(c) Before the secretary prints off the letter he does a *spell check*. It stops every time the year head's name, Mrs Smythe, appears.

What should he do to prevent this happening?

_____

_____

2. (continued)

(d) The secretary adds the graphic shown below to the letter.

He then makes changes so it looks like the graphic below.

Which features did he use?

1 _____

2 _____

(e) On seeing the letter the year head, Mrs Smythe, decides she would like to swap the last two paragraphs.

How could the secretary do this?

_____

_____

_____

(f) When creating the letters for parents both *program* and *data files* are used. Give an example of each type of file in this situation.

(i) Program file _____

(ii) Data file _____

(g) How is text represented in a computer system?

_____

[Turn over

3. A *spreadsheet* is kept of the money pupils have saved towards the weekend. From this money they have to pay for an extra trip. Below is part of the spreadsheet.

	A	B	C	D	E	F	G
1	Team Building Weekend						
2							
3	Name	Saved in August	Saved in September	Saved in October	Total Saved	Cost of extra trip	Balance of savings
4	Sally Jones	15	15	20	50	10	40
5	Hilary Smith	10	15	30	55	10	45
6	John Dale	5	10	10	25	10	15
7	Kate Reid	15	5	5	25	10	15
8	David Hill	20	5	10	35	10	25

(a) What formula is used in cell E4?

_____

(b) What formula is used in cell G4?

_____

_____

(c) What would have to be done to display all the appropriate figures as money?

_____

_____

(d) The year head wants to include the registration class of each pupil. What must be done to the above table to allow this to happen?

_____

_____

(e) The spreadsheet is part of an *integrated package*.

What is an "integrated package"?

_____

_____

_____

3. **(continued)**

(f) Give **one** advantage of the spreadsheet and the database having a similar *HCI*.

_____

_____

1
0

(g) An operating system has several standard functions. Tick (✓) **two** functions which the operating system would carry out while the spreadsheet was in use.

Loads the data file into the computer ☐

Displays numbers as money ☐

Supplies electricity to the computer ☐

Checks to see which key has been pressed ☐

2
1
0

(h) Why might the year head, Mrs Smythe, want to create a chart from the spreadsheet figures?

_____

_____

1
0

(i) The secretary has used both *online help* and an *online tutorial* for the spreadsheet.

Write whether you think online help or an online tutorial has been used for each of the following.

Introduction lesson

_____

Making a column wider whilst using the program

_____

2
1
0

(j) The spreadsheet is to be printed using a *laser* printer. Give **one** benefit of a laser printer.

_____

1
0

[Turn over

KU	PS

4. Pupils in computing have written a program in Really Basic to help run the tuckshop on the team building weekend. Really Basic is a *high level* language.

(*a*) Give **two** common features of high level languages.

1 _____

_____

2 _____

_____

2
1
0

(*b*) The computer can only understand *machine code*.

What is "machine code"?

_____

_____

1
0

(*c*) The program uses a graphic. Computers represent graphics by a series of tiny dots on the screen.

What are these dots on the screen called?

_____

_____

1
0

(*d*) A pupil called Sarah who has been helping to create the program has difficulty in writing. She uses a voice recognition package to produce text.

(i) What input device is necessary for the voice recognition package?

_____

1
0

(ii) When using it why must she speak clearly?

_____

_____

_____

(iii) Sarah complains to the teacher that she cannot use all the words she normally does in everyday conversation.

Why can she not use all the words she would like to?

_____

_____

1
0

1
0

DO NOT
WRITE IN
THIS MARGIN

KU	PS

4. **(continued)**

(*e*) Pupils are to take a computer with them on the team building weekend, to run the tuckshop program.

(i) Suggest a suitable type of computer for this purpose.

_____

(ii) Give a reason for your answer.

_____

_____

[Turn over

5. Pupils use canoes on the team building weekend which are made on an automated production line that uses *robots*.

(*a*) Give **two** reasons why you think the production process was automated.

1 _____

_____

2 _____

_____

(*b*) The various parts of the canoe are brought to the production line by *mobile* robots. The floor gets very dirty.

How can the mobile robots be guided to the correct place?

_____

_____

_____

(*c*) Suggest one safety precaution that should be taken around mobile robots.

_____

_____

_____

(*d*) Parts of the production process involves mixing a fast acting glue from two ingredients. A sensor is used to ensure this happens at the correct temperature.

(i) What type of processing should be used for this? Tick (✓) **one** box.

Real time ☐

Batch ☐

Interactive ☐

(ii) Explain your answer.

_____

_____

5. **(continued)**

(*e*)   The robot arms on the production line can sense if parts are in the correct position for joining together.   If they are not, then the parts are repositioned.

(i)   Is this an example of an *open* or *closed loop*?

_____

(ii)   Explain your answer.

_____

_____

(*f*)   The sensor is used to measure the level of light.

Is light a *digital* or *analogue* quantity?

_____

(*g*)   A large amount of data is constantly recorded during the production process and used frequently.

(i)   What is the best form of *backing storage* medium for this?   Choose from the list below.

CD ROM   *Hard Disk*   *Floppy Disk*   *Magnetic Tape*

_____

(ii)   Give a reason for your answer.

_____

_____

[Turn over

6. The organisation which provides the team building weekend buys their uniforms from a mail order company. Here is an example of an order form.

Order Form	
Customer Name:	Jessica Murray
Order Number:	3419
Date of Order:	130604
Product Code:	U789
Uniform Size:	32
Quantity:	4

Daily orders are gathered for processing overnight.

(*a*)　(i)　What type of processing is the company using?

_____

(ii)　Explain your answer.

_____

_____

_____

(*b*)　Checks are carried out by the computer as data is entered from the order form.

Name a field and suggest a suitable check.

Field name _____

Check _____

_____

(*c*)　What type of computer file will the order go into when first received? Tick (✓) **one** box.

Transaction　　☐

Master　　☐

Backup File　　☐

6. **(continued)**

(d)   The team building organisation pays the mail order company by cheque. The cheque has *MICR* characters on it.

   (i)   What do the initials MICR stand for?

_____

   (ii)   What is **one** advantage of MICR?

_____

(e)   One member of staff of the mail order company works from home.

Give **one** advantage and **one** disadvantage of working from home.

Advantage _____

_____

Disadvantage _____

_____

(f)   The mail order company sells mailing lists of its customers to other mail order companies. This causes junk mail.

Give **one** disadvantage of junk mail.

_____

_____

[END OF QUESTION PAPER]

[BLANK PAGE]

[BLANK PAGE]

C

0560/403

NATIONAL
QUALIFICATIONS
2005

THURSDAY, 12 MAY
10.35 AM – 12.20 PM

COMPUTING STUDIES
STANDARD GRADE
Credit Level

Read each question carefully.

Attempt **all** questions.

Write your answers in the answer book provided. **Do not** write on the question paper.

Write as neatly as possible.

Answer in sentences wherever possible.

SCOTTISH
QUALIFICATIONS
AUTHORITY

©

		KU	PS

1. FoneU is a chain of retail outlets that sells mobile phone packages. When a customer purchases a new phone, their details are entered into the company's database. The format of the database is shown below.

Field	Sample Data	Field Size (bytes)
Name	Summers, Heather	30
Address	9 Park Croft	60
Town	Newton	20
Postcode	PH40 3TS	8
Phone Make	Sunyo	15
Phone Model	AS300	5
Phone No	07793030181	12
Network	Talkfone	10

(a) (i) What is the maximum number of bytes required to store **one** record of the database?

1

(ii) Using your answer from part (i), calculate how many 1·44 Mb floppy disks will be needed to store 10,000 records.
Show all of your working.

4

(b) As the *data user*, the manager of FoneU has to comply with the *Data Protection Act* of 1998.

(i) Give **two** requirements of the Data Protection Act with which the data user must comply.

2

(ii) Give **two** rights that the *data subjects* have under this legislation.

2

(c) The sales manager wishes to send a *standard letter* to all customers living in Newtown who are on the Talkfone network.

(i) What is a standard letter?

2

(ii) Describe how the database could be used to produce a list of Talkfone customers living in Newtown.

3

(iii) What is the name given to the process of using a computer to insert the customers' details from the database into the standard letter in a single operation?

1

		KU	PS

	KU	PS

2. SubSea Contractors own a fleet of ships that are used to service oilrigs. One of their main tasks is to transfer drinking water from the ship's tanks to the oilrig. This is a computerised system, with software used to control the action of the ship's water pumps.

(a) Give **one** advantage of using a computerised system rather than a manual system in this case.　　　**1**

(b) Information about the water level is fed back to the system and the water pumps slow down, then stop when the water levels have reached a certain limit.

　(i) What do we call a device that is used to provide *feedback*?　　**1**

　(ii) The water levels vary continuously. What must be done to ensure that the water level readings are in a form that the computer system can process?　　　**1**

　(iii) What type of control loop is used in this situation?　　　**1**

(c) The software was written using a *control language* and is stored on *ROM chips*.

　(i) Give **one** reason why a control language was used for this system.　　　**1**

　(ii) Although ROM chips are the most expensive way of storing programs, give **two** reasons why this storage medium is used here.　　　**2**

(d) Workers onboard ship contact their families using *e-mail* on the ship's computer system. Which **two** of the following statements are true?

　A　A piece of software called a modem is needed for Internet access.
　B　ISPs can provide e-mail accounts.
　C　The computer's operating system is **not** involved in Internet access.
　D　Communications and Browser software is needed for Internet access.　　**2**

(e) This computer, like all others, has a *Central Processing Unit* (CPU) containing an *ALU* and a *Control Unit*.

　Explain the purpose of:

　(i) the ALU;　　**2**

　(ii) the Control Unit.　　**1**

[Turn over

	KU	PS

3. A Young Enterprise group hopes to raise money by selling two types of customised T-shirt. They use a spreadsheet to calculate what customers spend on their products.

Part of the spreadsheet is shown below.

	A	B	C	D	E	F
1	**Discount is**	20%				
2						
3	Name	T-shirt 1	T-shirt 2	Total	Discount	Final Cost
4	Kelly, J	10.00	5.00	15.00	3.00	12.00
5	Patel, R	3.00	7.00	10.00	0.00	10.00
6	McLean, A	3.00	3.00	6.00	0.00	6.00
7	Winters, H	8.00	3.00	11.00	2.20	8.80
8						
9						

(a) Cell **D4** contains a formula to calculate the total amount owed. It has been *replicated* into cells **D5**, **D6** and **D7**.

   (i) What is meant by the term "replicate"?   **1**

   (ii) Which type of *referencing* would have been used to replicate this formula?   **1**

(b) If customers spend over £10, then a discount of 20% is given. Cell **E4** uses a formula to calculate any discount due.

   (i) Write down a suitable formula for cell **E4** **which includes** cell **B1**.   **4**

   (ii) Before this formula was replicated down column **E**, one of the cells in the formula required an *absolute reference*. Which cell?   **1**

   (iii) What could be done to prevent the formula in this column from being altered unintentionally?   **1**

(c) The *cell attributes* of **B4** to **F7** are to be changed.

   (i) What is meant by the term cell attributes?   **1**

   (ii) Suggest a suitable alteration to the cell attributes.   **1**

(d) Every month the Young Enterprise group produces a word processed report showing sales for that month. It includes a table similar to that shown above. Should *static* or *dynamic data linkage* be used in this case? Justify your answer.   **2**

	KU	PS

	KU	PS

4. MegaTrain is a call-centre company that sells thousands of tickets each day for train journeys throughout the UK. Each employee uses a *remote terminal* connected to a mainframe computer at the company's head office in Manchester. This computer has a large database that holds information about the trains and ticket availability. Employees use this database to inform customers of prices and book seats when required.

An excerpt from the database is shown below.

Train Code	Depart	Destination	Total Seats	Seats Sold	Seats Available
31243	Waverley	Queen Street	350	295	55
31255	Waverley	Kings Cross	800	451	349
32453	Central	Euston	800	704	96

(a) The value in the field "Seats Available" is automatically generated by the computer. What name is given to this type of field?   **1**

(b) The last digit in the field "Train Code" is a *check digit*.

   (i) What is the purpose of a check digit?   **1**

   (ii) From what data is the check digit calculated?   **1**

(c) Should this database be stored on *random (direct) access* backing storage media or *sequential access* backing storage media? Explain your answer.   **2**

(d) MegaTrain makes daily backup copies of the database. Three generations of backup are kept. Describe this backup process. (You may use a diagram.)   **3**

(e) The mainframe computer allows *multi-access* from its remote terminals.

   (i) What is a remote terminal?   **1**

   (ii) Explain what is meant by the term multi-access.   **2**

   (iii) Why is a multi-access system required at MegaTrain?   **1**

(f) MegaTrain customers generally pay for their tickets over the phone using *electronic funds transfer* (*EFT*).

What steps are involved in the process of electronic funds transfer?   **3**

(g) Morven, an employee at MegaTrain, has poor eyesight. The *HCI parameters* of her remote terminal have been altered to make it easier for her to see what is on the screen.

Describe **two** ways in which the parameters may have been changed.   **2**

[Turn over

	KU	PS

5. Ben has his own business, selling classroom resources to teachers. He needs software to help him construct letters and calculate his expenditure.

(a) He is unsure whether to buy an *integrated package* or separate *general purpose packages*.

Give **two** reasons why he may decide to buy separate general purpose packages. **2**

(b) Before he makes his purchase, Ben has to ensure his computer is capable of running the new software.

Name **two** features of his computer system that he will have to check to see whether it is able to run this software. **2**

(c) Ben has designed a unique company logo for all his correspondence.

Name the legislation that makes copying Ben's work, without his permission, an offence. **1**

(d) Some of his products are software packages that teachers can use for training purposes. They are distributed to schools on *CD-ROM*. He has tried to make these products as *user friendly* as possible by including *online help* and *online tutorials*.

  (i) What is online help? **1**

  (ii) What is an online tutorial? **1**

  (iii) He has also designed the software so that it is *portable*.

    What is meant by the term portable? **1**

  (iv) Give **two** reasons for using CD-ROM as a distribution medium. **2**

(e) Ben has bought a new computer. The *operating system* offers *multi-programming* and efficient *resource allocation*.

  (i) What is meant by the term multi-programming? **2**

  (ii) Why is resource allocation an essential role of the operating system? **2**

  (iii) Another role of the operating system is to manage *main memory*.

    How does the operating system locate items in main memory? **2**

[END OF QUESTION PAPER]

FOR OFFICIAL USE

G

	KU	PS
Total Marks		

0560/402

NATIONAL QUALIFICATIONS 2006

THURSDAY, 11 MAY
G/C 9.00 AM – 10.15 AM
F/**G** 10.20 AM – 11.35 AM

COMPUTING STUDIES STANDARD GRADE
General Level

Fill in these boxes and read what is printed below.

Full name of centre

Town

Forename(s)

Surname

Date of birth

Day Month Year   Scottish candidate number   Number of seat

Read each question carefully.

Attempt **all** questions.

Write your answers in the space provided on the question paper.

Write as neatly as possible.

Answer in sentences wherever possible.

Before leaving the examination room you must give this book to the invigilator. If you do not, you may lose all the marks for this paper.

SCOTTISH
QUALIFICATIONS
AUTHORITY

©

1. A new community centre is soon to open in the town of Bishophill. The manager is creating a web page to advertise the centre.

   (a) Apart from text, name **two** other *types of data* which could be included in the web page.

   _____

   _____

   (b) State **one** method which can be used to prepare web pages.

   _____

   _____

   (c) The manager wants readers of the web page to be able to go directly to a page, which already exists, on the history of the town.

   Describe **one** way in which this could be done.

   _____

   _____

   (d) A group of school children are designing a logo for the community centre, using a drawing package. A line in the logo looked like this.

   It has been changed to look like the one below.

   What has happened to make this change?

   _____

   _____

1. (continued)

(e) The community centre intends holding music evening classes.

Using the Internet, the manager wants to find out what other music evening classes are available in the town of Bishophill.

Tick (✓) the **one** option which would let him find this out most efficiently.

Use a search engine and search for evening classes. ☐

Type in the individual address of each known evening class provider. ☐

Use a search engine and search for music evening classes and Bishophill. ☐

1
0

[Turn over

2. A letter is being sent out to everyone who has registered an interest in the community centre. The letter contains a *standard paragraph*.

(*a*)   (i)   What is a standard paragraph?

_____

_____

2
1
0

(ii)   State **one** advantage of a standard paragraph.

_____

_____

1
0

(*b*)   What feature of the word processing software would pick up the following underlined mistake?

The centre <u>are</u> having an opening ceremony on 27 September 2006.

_____

1
0

(*c*)   The letter is to include a timetable of the various activities taking place in the community centre.

Describe **two** reasons why the *table* facility would prove useful in this situation.

1 _____

_____

2 _____

_____

2
1
0

(*d*)   Page two of the letter starts in the middle of a paragraph.

What facility within a word processing package can be used to force the whole paragraph to move onto page two?

_____

_____

1
0

3. Below is a record from the database which holds details of people who have registered an interest in the community centre.

Registration Number	156
Name	Cameron Murray
Date of Birth	04/03/86
Sex	Male
Address line 1	13 Fauld Street
Address line 2	Bishophill
Postcode	BH3 82Y
Main Interest	Music

(a) Look at the above record and write down **two** *field types* that could be used in this database.

1 _____

2 _____

2
1
0

(b) What type of check could be done on the Date of Birth field to ensure that it falls within the years 1905 to 2006?

_____

1
0

(c) How could the database be used to identify the youngest person who has registered an interest in the community centre?

_____

_____

2
1
0

(d) Complete the following paragraph which describes how you would obtain a paper copy of people born after 01/07/85 and who are interested in music.

Perform a complex _____ on the "Date of Birth" field for a

date _____ 01/07/85 AND the _____ field

for "Music". Produce a paper copy using a _____ .

4
3
2
1
0

[Turn over

4. The manager of the community centre has made a spreadsheet of the various activities that are planned.

	A	B	C	D	E	F	G
1	Activity	Number of Participants	Cost per Participant	Total from Participants	Tutor Fee	Cost of Room	Profit
2	Beginners French	12	£55.55	£666.60	£200.00	£60.50	£406.10
3	5-a-side football	10	£20.00	£200.00	£50.00	£100.00	£50.00
4	Learn to play Guitar	6	£75.00	£450.00	£70.00	£60.50	£319.50
5	Painting	20	£35.00	£700.00	£200.00	£80.00	£420.00
6							
7							
8							
9	Maximum attending a class	20					
10	Average Tutor fee	£130.00					
11							

(a) What can be done to prevent the Tutor Fee from being changed accidentally?

_____

(b) Tick (✓) **one** box which gives the formula which is in G2.

= B2*C2 ☐

= D2–E2+F2 ☐

= D2+E2 ☐

= D2–E2–F2 ☐

(c) In cells B9 and B10 functions have been used. Fill in the spaces below with the functions and cell references in the appropriate places.

(i) B9 = _____ (_____ : _____)

(ii) B10 = _____ (_____ : _____)

(d) The manager wants a printout for the notice board of the number of people taking part in each activity.

State **one** reason why he might present the figures as a *chart* for this printout.

_____

_____

KU	PS

5. The manager of the community centre is working out a budget for the running of the office.

   (*a*)   Describe **two** *running costs* of computers.

        1 _____

        2 _____

2
1
0

   (*b*)   The manager also has to consider *security* with regard to the use of computers.

      Suggest **two** methods which could be used to *control access* to the data held on computers.

        1 _____

          _____

        2 _____

          _____

2
1
0

   (*c*)   It can be argued that computers are expensive to buy. State **one** other disadvantage of introducing computers to an office.

        _____

        _____

1
0

[Turn over

KU	PS

KU | PS

6. Within the reception area of the community centre there is going to be a computer which runs an *expert system*. This expert system is to give advice as to which activities people may be interested in.

(*a*)   (i)   Where else might an expert system be used?

_____

_____

1 0

(ii)   What would it be used for in this situation?

_____

_____

1 0

(*b*)   People may wish to take a printout of the results from the expert system. The manager must purchase a new printer for this.

Suggest **one** reason why he might choose to buy **each** of the following printers.

Laser _____

_____

Inkjet _____

_____

2 1 0

(*c*)   Expert systems are written in *high level languages*. Why is it necessary for high level languages to be *translated*?

_____

_____

1 0

(*d*)   Apart from translation, state **two** *common features* of high level languages.

_____

_____

_____

_____

2 1 0

KU | PS

KU	PS

6. (continued)

(e)   Live images of what is happening in reception are to be displayed on the community centre's web page.

Suggest an input device which could be used to capture these images.

_____

(f)   The computers in the community centre have *LCDs* which use *TFT* technology.

(i)   What do the initials LCD stand for?

L _____ C_____ D_____

(ii)   What do the initials TFT stand for?

T _____ F_____ T_____

[Turn over

7. When a person calls to book a place for an evening class, the receptionist checks the computer for availability and can respond by making the booking.

(*a*) What type of processing is this?

_____

1
0

(*b*) The centre creates a membership code for each member. Below is an example of a membership code and how it is created.

Write beside each one whether it is *data* or *information*.

(i) Code: CM1986M _____

2
1
0

(ii) How it is created:

CM	1986	M
Initials	DOB	Sex

_____

(*c*) The membership code, shown above, is held in the community centre's computer.

Tick (✓) **one** box which describes how the membership code will be represented within the computer's memory.

Bitmap ▢

ASCII ▢

Graphics ▢

1
0

(*d*) The person then sends in a cheque to pay for their evening class. The cheque contains *Magnetic Ink Character Recognition (MICR)* characters.

Describe **two** advantages of MICR.

1 _____

_____

2 _____

2
1
0

_____

7. (continued)

(e) Later that week the person goes on to their *on-line banking* to see whether the cheque has been taken off their bank balance. To access on-line banking a *password* must be used.

(i) Tick (✓) **one** box which best describes a safe and suitable password.

Your name ☐

Your date of birth ☐

A combination of letters and numbers ☐

Two letters of the alphabet ☐

(ii) State **one** reason why people using on-line banking should be glad of the Computer Misuse Act.

_____

_____

_____

(f) In years to come the community centre may expand greatly and require the services of a *Network Manager*.

Tick (✓) **one** box to indicate a specific duty of a Network Manager.

Deciding each user's level of access ☐

Writing a program ☐

Repairing a computer ☐

(g) The centre manager is worried about information stored in a database being lost or damaged.

What would you suggest he does?

_____

_____

[Turn over

DO NOT
WRITE IN
THIS MARGIN

KU	PS

7. (continued)

(*h*) The manager uses both *data files* and *program files*. The membership file is a data file.

Tick (✓) the most appropriate definition for each.

(i) **Program file**   A set of instructions ☐

A file created by or used within a program ☐

1
0

(ii) **Data file**   A set of instructions ☐

A file created or used within a program ☐

1
0

8. When e-mailing tutors who are going to take classes at the community centre the manager must be aware of *netiquette*.

(*a*)　(i)　What is meant by the term *netiquette*?

_____

_____

1
0

(ii)　Give **two** examples of rules used in *netiquette*.

1 _____

_____

2 _____

_____

2
1
0

(*b*)　The manager currently uses a *dial-up connection* and wants to move to a *broadband connection*.

Give **two** advantages of using broadband.

1 _____

_____

2 _____

_____

2
1
0

[Turn over

KU	PS

9. The community centre will be holding a trip to a theme park. One of the rides involves passengers travelling back in time in a car (an automated vehicle) through Dinosaurland.

(a) One dinosaur breathes fire as it detects cars going past. Suggest a suitable device which could be used to detect the cars.

_____

(b) Sound effects are used as part of this ride.

Is sound an analogue or digital quantity?

_____

_____

(c) There is an emergency stop button in each car. This sends information back to the main computer which will then stop all other cars which are following on behind.

Why is real time processing necessary in this situation?

_____

_____

(d) Riders cannot control the route they take. These automated vehicles do not run on rails.

Describe another method for guiding an automated vehicle.

_____

_____

_____

_____

(e) Before automated vehicles were used people were employed to drive cars around Dinosaurland.

Give **one** advantage to the owners of the theme park of the cars being automated.

_____

_____

9. **(continued)**

(f) During the ride people can look at a black and white map of Dinosaurland, which is displayed on a monitor within the car.

  (i) Explain how the computer stores a black and white image in memory.

    _____

    _____

  (ii) Using your answer to the question above, how would you expect the following shape to be stored in the computer's memory? Complete Diagram B using binary numbers.

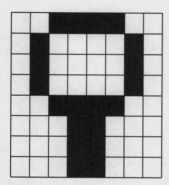

Diagram A: Image displayed on screen

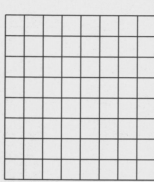

Diagram B: Image stored in computer's memory

(g) Suggest **one** way in which this ride could be simulated in other theme parks.

    _____

    _____

    _____

[END OF QUESTION PAPER]

[BLANK PAGE]

[BLANK PAGE]

FOR OFFICIAL USE

C

Total Marks | KU | PS |

0560/403

NATIONAL
QUALIFICATIONS
2006

THURSDAY, 11 MAY
10.35 AM – 12.20 PM

**COMPUTING STUDIES
STANDARD GRADE**
Credit Level

Fill in these boxes and read what is printed below.

Full name of centre

Town

Forename(s)

Surname

Date of birth

Day Month Year

Scottish candidate number

Number of seat

Read each question carefully.

Attempt **all** questions.

Write your answers in the space provided on the question paper.

Write as neatly as possible.

Answer in sentences wherever possible.

Before leaving the examination room you must give this book to the invigilator. If you do not, you may lose all the marks for this paper.

SCOTTISH
QUALIFICATIONS
AUTHORITY

SA 0560/403 6/14070

1. Pupils and staff at Kulross Academy are about to move into a purpose-built, brand-new school.

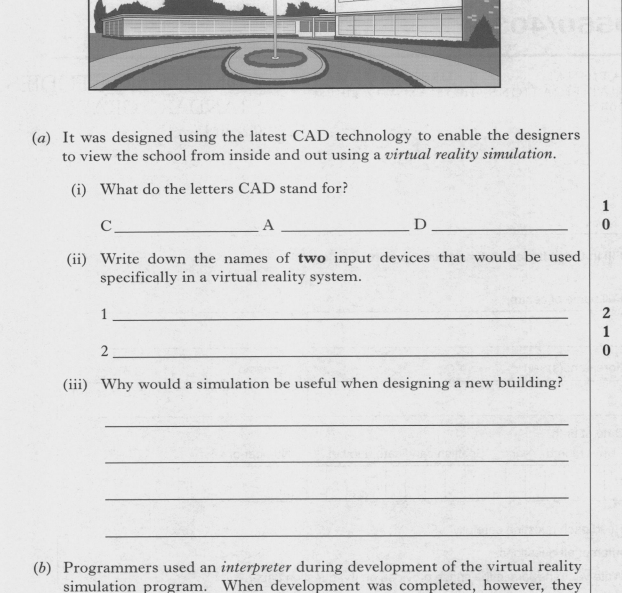

(*a*) It was designed using the latest CAD technology to enable the designers to view the school from inside and out using a *virtual reality simulation*.

(i) What do the letters CAD stand for?

C_____ A _____ D _____

(ii) Write down the names of **two** input devices that would be used specifically in a virtual reality system.

1 _____

2 _____

(iii) Why would a simulation be useful when designing a new building?

_____

_____

_____

_____

(*b*) Programmers used an *interpreter* during development of the virtual reality simulation program. When development was completed, however, they used a *compiler*.

(i) What are interpreters and compilers used for?

_____

_____

Page two

1. **(b)** **(continued)**

(ii) Why might programmers use an interpreter first, and then on completion use a compiler?

_____

_____

_____

_____

(c) The completed program was distributed **by post** to parents, pupils and staff, to allow them to preview the school before building work began.

(i) What distribution medium is most likely to have been used?

(Tick (✓) **one** box.)

CD-ROM [ ]   USB *flash drive* [ ]   *Floppy disk* [ ]

(ii) Explain why the other two media are not suitable.

1 _____

_____

2 _____

_____

[Turn over

2. At the opening ceremony, guests were given a demonstration of the school's technological facilities.

(a) Distributed throughout the school are *terminals* showing the school's intranet. *Hyperlinks* and *hotspots* are activated using the mouse pointer.

(i) What is a "hyperlink"?

_____

_____

(ii) How can users tell that the intranet page has hotspots?

_____

_____

(b) All desktop and laptop computers are networked throughout the school. The network is a *client-server* network.

(i) What is a client in a network?

_____

(ii) What is the purpose of a server in such a network?

_____

_____

(c) Some computers within the school are linked to the server via *wireless* technology, while others are connected to the server using cables.

(i) State **one** advantage of using cables.

_____

_____

(ii) State **one** advantage of using wireless technology.

_____

_____

KU	PS

2. **(c) (continued)**

    (iii) Describe **one** disadvantage of the use of wireless technology.

_____

_____

    (iv) All computers in this network have been fitted with a special card that enables communication with the server.

        What is this card called?

_____

_____

(d) The server has a processor, containing a *control unit, ALU* and *registers*.

    (i) What is the function of the ALU?

_____

_____

_____

    (ii) What is the function of the registers?

_____

_____

_____

[Turn over

KU	PS

Margin marks: 10, 10, 210, 10

3. Kulross Academy features a unique *mobile robot* that patrols the corridors during lessons, keeping them free of litter.

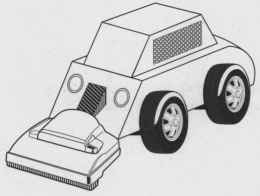

(*a*) The designers originally planned to use a *light guidance system* for the robot to 'find' its way along the corridors. However, they decided to use a *magnetic guidance system* with *real-time processing* instead.

(i) What is meant by "real-time processing"?

_____

_____

(ii) Explain why they decided not to use a light guidance system following a painted line on the floor?

_____

_____

_____

(*b*) The safety of pupils and teachers is extremely important. Each robot is fitted with multiple bump *sensors* which cause the robot to stop if it detects any pressure.

(i) Is this an example of an *intelligent robot*? _____

(ii) Explain your answer.

_____

_____

_____

_____

3.   (continued)

(c) The program controlling the robot was written using a *control language* and is stored in *ROM* within the robot.

(i)   Describe what is meant by a control language.

_____

_____

_____

(ii) Describe **one** advantage of storing software on ROM.

_____

_____

_____

[Turn over

4. Another new feature of Kulross Academy is the use of identity cards, with all staff being issued with *smart cards*.

(*a*) Which of the following statements are true: (Tick (✓) **two** boxes only.)

1. Smart cards have their own processor. ☐

2. It is easy to forge smart cards. ☐

3. Smart cards are also known as mark sense cards. ☐

4. The information on a smart card can be updated. ☐

(*b*) When they are first issued with smart cards, teachers have to enter a 4-digit pin number. *Verification* is carried out at this stage.

(i) What is the purpose of verification?

_____

_____

(ii) How could the 4-digit pin number be verified?

_____

_____

(*c*) Pupils use magnetic stripe cards for registration and payment of school lunches. When a pupil enters a classroom, the card is passed through a special piece of hardware.

What is this hardware called?

_____

(*d*) When a pupil 'purchases' food from any of the school's dining facilities, details of the purchase are logged in a database on the school's computer network.

(i) Many dining staff may be accessing this database at one time.

What is the term used to describe such a database?

M _____ U _____ Database

4.   (***d***) **(continued)**

    (ii) Data can be accessed in two ways – *randomly* or *sequentially*. Which type of access would be appropriate in this situation? Explain your answer.

       Type _____

       Explanation _____

       _____

       _____

       _____

(***e***) The school's computer network holds lots of personal data about both staff and pupils. The *data controller* must make sure that the data is accurate and kept up to date.

    (i) Describe **two** other responsibilities that the data controller has.

      1 _____

      _____

      2 _____

      _____

    (ii) The *data subjects* also have rights. Who are the data subjects in this case?

      _____

      _____

[Turn over

5.   A competition was held to design a new crest for the school. The winning entry is shown below:

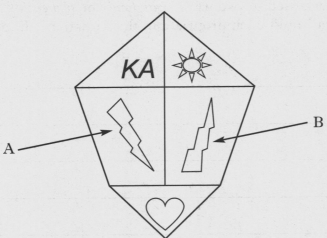

(a) Object A of the image has been copied to create object B.

Describe what else has happened to the copied image.

_____

_____

(b) The image is scanned and part of the image is *cropped*.

Explain what is meant by cropping a graphic.

_____

_____

(c) The image is stored as a *black and white bit-mapped graphic,* measuring 450 pixels wide by 600 pixels high.

Calculate the storage requirements in kilobytes.

(Show all working.)

_____

_____

_____

_____

_____

5. **(continued)**

(*d*) The graphic is to be distributed electronically to **all** teachers throughout the school. This can be done in two ways:

1. Sent as an *attachment* using electronic mail.

2. Stored in a read/write shared area of the network that teachers and pupils can access.

  (i)   What is an attachment?

_____

_____

  (ii)   Describe **one** advantage of sending the graphic as an attachment.

_____

_____

  (iii)   Describe **one** disadvantage of distributing the graphic using the shared area.

_____

_____

[Turn over

6. A Maths teacher at Kulross Academy uses a spreadsheet to store his pupils' test results. Part of the spreadsheet is shown below:

	A	B	C	D	E	F
1	Name	Test1	Test2	Test3	Average	Letter home?
2	Ben Adams	53	67	63	61	No
3	Paula Bryant	35	33	31	33	Yes
4	Nasim Collins	76	81	93	83	No
5	Darren Daly	23	56	18	32	Yes
6	Lucy Locke	78	72	86	79	No

(a) Cell E2 contains a *function* to calculate the average. It has been *replicated* from E2 into cells E3 to E6.

　(i) What is meant by replication?

_____

_____

　(ii) Has *relative* or *absolute* replication been used in this case? Explain your answer.

　Type of Replication _____

　Explanation _____

_____

_____

_____

(b) The teacher is concerned with the progress of some of his pupils. If a pupil's average result is less than 50, then he intends to send a letter home informing parents of his concern.

Cell F2 contains a function that automatically identifies the pupils. Part of the function is shown below. Complete the function.

= _____ (E2 < 50, "Yes", _____)

6. **(continued)**

(c) The Maths teacher finds it time consuming having to create lots of similar letters. His colleague, a Computing teacher, recommends he creates a *standard letter*.

She suggests that the original letter can be scanned into the computer using *OCR*.

(i) What is meant by "OCR"?

O_____ C _____ R _____

(ii) What is a standard letter?

_____

_____

(iii) What is the process called when information from a data file is inserted into a standard letter?

_____

(iv) A *template* could also be used to speed up creation of the letters.

What is a "template"?

_____

_____

(d) The Computing teacher also recommends that the finished letter is stored as an *RTF* file format.

(i) What is meant by "RTF"?

R_____ T _____ F _____

(ii) Describe **one** advantage of storing a file as an RTF file type.

_____

_____

_____

Margin marks: 1 0 ; 2 1 0 ; 1 0 (PS); 2 1 0 ; 1 0 (KU); 1 0 (PS)

[Turn over

7. The *Network Manager* at Kulross Academy keeps a database of all computer software in the school. Part of the database is shown below.

Name	Date of Purchase	Location	Computer ID	Type
DT Publishing	05-11-05	ICT Rm 1	333	Freeware
DT Publishing	05-11-05	ICT Rm 2	456	Freeware
DT Publishing	10-01-06	ICT Rm 2	342	Freeware
WordPlus	20-05-05	CDT Rm 32	654	Shareware
WordPlus	20-05-05	CDT Rm 32	765	Commercial
WordPlus	20-05-05	CDT Rm 32	875	Shareware
WYNIP	03-04-06	ICT Rm 2	458	Shareware
WYNIP	03-04-06	ICT Rm 1	567	Shareware

Kulross Academy - Software Inventory

(*a*) It has been sorted, in a complex way, on three fields.

Identify the fields in the **order** in which the sort occurs. The first one has been done for you.

FIELD 1. Name

FIELD 2. _____

FIELD 3. _____

2
1
0

(*b*) The network manager wishes to produce a list of all Shareware that was installed before the 1 April 2006. Describe how this could be done.

_____

_____

_____

_____

3
2
1
0

(*c*) Many databases make use of *computed fields*. When would a computed field be used in a database?

_____

_____

1
0

KU	PS

7. **(continued)**

   (d) What is *shareware*?

   _____

   _____

   _____

   1
   0

   (e) What is *freeware*?

   _____

   _____

   _____

   1
   0

   (f) Sometimes pupils try to install games, without permission, on to the school network.

   State the name of the piece of legislation which makes this action illegal.

   _____

   _____

   1
   0

   [Turn over

8. At the end of their first year at Kulross Academy, some pupils decide to create a multimedia presentation highlighting the successes of the new school.

   (*a*) The name of the school as well as the new crest will appear in the same position on every slide of the presentation, as shown below.

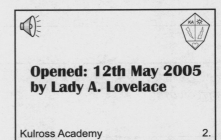

   Explain how this could be done.

   _____

   _____

   _____

   _____

   (*b*) The presentation will also contain sound and other images.

   (i) State **one** way of *capturing audio* for the presentation.

   _____

   _____

   (ii) State **one** way of *capturing images* for the presentation.

   _____

   _____

   (*c*) What makes this presentation *multimedia*?

   _____

   _____

   _____

   [*END OF QUESTION PAPER*]

[BLANK PAGE]

FOR OFFICIAL USE

G

KU   PS

Total Marks

0560/402

NATIONAL QUALIFICATIONS 2007

WEDNESDAY, 2 MAY
G/C 9.00 AM –10.15 AM
F/G 10.20 AM –11.35 AM

COMPUTING STUDIES STANDARD GRADE
General Level

Fill in these boxes and read what is printed below.

Full name of centre

Town

Forename(s)

Surname

Date of birth

Day Month Year   Scottish candidate number   Number of seat

Read each question carefully.

Attempt **all** questions.

Write your answers in the space provided on the question paper.

Write as neatly as possible.

Answer in sentences wherever possible.

Before leaving the examination room you must give this book to the invigilator. If you do not, you may lose all the marks for this paper.

SCOTTISH
QUALIFICATIONS
AUTHORITY
©

1. The Gibson family are going on holiday to a Scottish island.
   They are travelling by car and ferry.

   (a) The family find out more about the ferry crossing by going *on-line* at
   www.scotferry.co.uk.

   What does the "www" stand for at the beginning of the address?

   W _____ W _____ W _____

   (b) The ferry company sends the Gibsons a letter confirming their booking.
   At the bottom of the letter is a *standard paragraph*.

   What is a standard paragraph?

   _____

   _____

   _____

   (c) The company's stationery looks like this:

   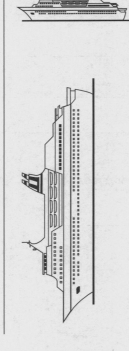

   Scotland by Ferry
   Ship Road
   Ullapool

   State the changes that have been made to the graphic at the top to make it
   look like the one at the side.

   _____

   _____

1. (continued)

(d) Throughout the letter, Gibson has been typed as "Gibbson".

What feature of the word processing package could be used to correct this mistake in **one operation**?

_____

(e) The ferry company has enclosed details of its crossings.

Journey	Departure	Arrival
Ullapool – Stornoway	0900	1130
Ullapool – Summer Islands	1030	1110

State **two** advantages in using the *table* facility to create this layout.

1 _____

_____

2 _____

_____

[Turn over

2. The Ferry Company keep a spreadsheet for each crossing.

	A	B	C	D	E	F
1	**Ferry Crossings 2007**					
2						
3	**Journey**	**Number of passengers**	**Cost per passenger**	**Number of cars**	**Cost per car**	**Total from passengers and cars**
4	Ullapool to Stornoway	300	£13.00	98	£23.00	£6,154.00
5	Ullapool to Summer Islands	150	£7.50	30	£15.00	£1,575.00
6	Oban to Mull	60	£8.00	52	£20.00	£1,520.00
7						
8						
9	Average number of cars per sailing			60		

KU | PS

(a) Cell F4 contains a formula. Part of it is shown below. Complete the formula.

= (_____ * _____) + (_____ * _____)

2 1 0

(b) Cell D9 contains a function. Part of it is shown below. Complete the function.

= _____ (_____ : _____)

2 1 0

(c) State **two** ways in which cell A3 has been formatted.

1 _____

2 _____

2 1 0

(d) What *attribute* has been applied to the numbers in cells C4 to C6?

_____

1 0

3. One of the children in the Gibson family gets seasick on ferry journeys. Mrs Gibson notices that her local chemist has an *expert system*, which covers various illnesses including travel sickness.

(*a*) What is an expert system?

_____

_____

_____

210

(*b*) State **one** area, other than medicine, where an expert system could be used and what it could be used for in that **area**.

Area _____

What it would be used for _____

_____

_____

20

(*c*) On board the ferry there is a *multimedia* presentation about the island.

(i) State **one** reason for using *audio* in a presentation.

_____

_____

10

(ii) A *hyperlink* is used between slides in the presentation.

What is a hyperlink?

_____

_____

10

(iii) On one of the islands it is possible to go white water rafting. The presentation includes this as a *video* clip.

State **one** reason for using a video clip in a presentation rather than a photograph.

_____

_____

10

[Turn over

4. (a) The ferry company uses a *database* to keep a file of all its customers. For each of the fields below state a suitable *field type*.

The first one has been done for you.

Field Name	Example	Field Type
Name	Harry Gibson	Text
Address	3 Ballater Drive	_____
Age	36	_____
Outward Journey	13/10/07	_____

(b) Below is part of a record from the customer file.

Name	Harry Gibson
Customer Code	HG3679
Departure	Ullapool
Destination	Stornoway
Outward Journey	13/10/07
Time	1830 hours
Type of Car	Land Ranger

The ferry company wishes to know how many Land Rangers are travelling from Ullapool to Stornoway on 13/10/07.

Choose **five** words from the list below to complete the paragraph.

Search   *Sort*   *Name*   *Stornoway*   *Ullapool*

Destination   *AND*   *13/10/07*   *OR*

Perform a complex _____ on

fields Departure equals _____

AND _____ equals Stornoway

_____ Outward Journey equals _____

AND Type of Car equals Land Ranger.

KU PS

3
2
1
0

4
3
2
1
0

DO NOT
WRITE IN
THIS MARGIN

| KU | PS |

4. (continued)

(c) The company now wish to put this list in alphabetical order

- firstly by name

- and then by type of car.

Number the steps below to show the correct order.

[ ]   and choose to sort on type of car

[ ]   start a new complex sort

[ ]   choose to sort on customer name

2
1
0

(d) When a customer's code is typed in, the computer checks that only six characters have been entered.

What *type of check* is this?

_____

1
0

(e) Only certain employees should have access to the database.

Describe **two** suitable methods which they could use to control access.

1 _____

_____

2 _____

_____

2
1
0

(f) A passenger is surprised to receive a brochure from a holiday homes company which is based on the island they are travelling to.

Tick (✓) **one** box which indicates how the holiday homes company got their name and address.

The passenger wrote to the company   [ ]

The ferry company have sold their customer list   [ ]

1
0

[Turn over

| KU | PS |

5. The ferry has *sensors* on its doors which prevents the ferry from sailing if the doors are not sealed.

(*a*) (i) State the type of processing that is being used to control the ferry doors.

_____

(ii) State a reason for this.

_____

_____

(*b*) State a type of sensor which could be used in this situation.

_____

(*c*) The ferry sometimes has to transport cargo. Before loading, the cargo is kept in a warehouse. The warehouse uses automated vehicles which are guided by a light system.

Using **some** of the words below complete the paragraph about a light guidance system.

control   *feedback*   *sensor*   *magnet*   *instructions*

A _____ follows a white line. Should the vehicle move

away from the line _____ causes the computer to send

out _____ which bring it back to the correct position.

(*d*) State **two** advantages of using automated vehicles.

1 _____

_____

2 _____

_____

6. *(a)* Some people are very frightened of sailing. Describe how *virtual reality* could be used to overcome their fears.

_____

_____

_____

_____

2
1
0

(b) The shop on board the ferry uses a computer program for stock taking. It is written in a *high level language*.

Tick (✓) **two** boxes which are *common features* of high level languages.

Written in binary ☐

English like ☐

Portable ☐

Cannot be edited ☐

2
1
0

(c) Explain why it is necessary for high level languages to be translated.

_____

_____

_____

1
0

(d) How are numbers represented in a computer?

Tick (✓) **one** box.

ASCII ☐

Pixels ☐

Binary ☐

1
0

[Turn over

6. **(continued)**

(e) The shop saves information onto *backing storage*. Put the following types of backing storage into order, according to their *capacity*. One box has been completed for you.

Use **1** for the **smallest** and **4** for the **largest**.

USB Flash Drive   2

DVD Rewriteable   [ ]

Hard Drive   [ ]

CD Rewritable   [ ]

(f) The shop needs to make printouts of its stock taking. The printouts will include figures which must be able to be read clearly.

(i) Suggest a suitable type of printer.

_____

(ii) State **one** reason for your answer.

_____

_____

(g) Some passengers like to have a picture of themselves put onto a sheet of paper which shows the ferry and a map of the island.

Number the steps below from 1 to 4 to show the correct order of how this could be achieved. The **first step** should be **numbered 1**.

Import photograph to desk top publishing package   [ ]

Print document   [ ]

Take photograph of customer with digital camera   [ ]

Save document   [ ]

6. (continued)

(*h*) Within the shop there is a *monitor* which displays live pictures, with sound, of what is happening on the captain's bridge.

State **two** pieces of hardware, other than a monitor, which could be used to display the live pictures.

1 _____

2 _____

(*i*) The manageress of the shop often uses a *laptop* computer.

State the type of monitor a laptop would have.

_____

(*j*) The manageress uses her laptop to create adverts for the shop. Complete the following sentences using the words provided.

data   *program*

The manageress uses a desk top publishing package.

This is a _____ file.

With this she creates an advert. This is a _____ file.

[Turn over

7. (a) Working out how many cars could travel on the ferry used to be done manually. Now a computer program calculates it.

Who would have examined the old system to see if computerisation was possible? Tick (✓) **one** box.

Programmer ☐

Systems Analyst ☐

Engineer ☐

Network Manager ☐

(b) Use **some** of the following words to complete the sentences below.

programmer   *engineers*   *network manager*   *systems analyst*

When computers were first installed at the ferry company's head office

they were installed by _____ .

A _____ was employed to write a program which

calculates the weight on board the ferry.

There are now so many computers linked together it is necessary to

employ a _____ to allocate usernames.

(c) (i) Some customers pay for their ferry crossing using cheques which have *MICR (Magnetic Ink Character Recognition)* data printed on them.

State **one** advantage of MICR

_____

_____

(ii) Others use *EFT* to pay for their fare.

What do the initials EFT stand for?

E _____ F_____ T _____

8. (*a*) The following statements refer to *broadband* or *dial-up* connections.

Choose the appropriate type of connection for each statement.

The first one has been done for you.

		Broadband	**Dial-up**
1	Provides faster speed of access to the Internet.	✓	☐
2	This type of connection is always on.	☐	☐
3	This type of connection can be paid for by the minute.	☐	☐
4	Telephone calls can be made and received at the same time as being connected to the Internet.	☐	☐

(*b*) What does it mean to be *off-line*?

_____

_____

(*c*) The ferry company sends an *e-mail* to a customer which is written in CAPITAL LETTERS.

Why should they **not** have used capital letters?

_____

_____

(*d*) On board each ferry there is a *wireless Local Area Network*.

State **two** advantages of using wireless technology.

1 _____

_____

2 _____

_____

[END OF QUESTION PAPER]

[BLANK PAGE]

[BLANK PAGE]

FOR OFFICIAL USE

C

K!J   PS

Total Marks

0560/403

NATIONAL   WEDNESDAY, 2 MAY
QUALIFICATIONS   10.35 AM – 12.20 PM
2007

**COMPUTING STUDIES
STANDARD GRADE**
Credit Level

Fill in these boxes and read what is printed below.

Full name of centre

Town

Forename(s)

Surname

Date of birth

Day   Month   Year   Scottish candidate number   Number of seat

Read each question carefully.

Attempt **all** questions.

Write your answers in the space provided on the question paper.

Write as neatly as possible.

Answer in sentences wherever possible.

Before leaving the examination room you must give this book to the invigilator. If you do not, you may lose all the marks for this paper.

SCOTTISH
QUALIFICATIONS
AUTHORITY

SA 0560/403 6/16570   ©

1. Glencoe House is an outdoor centre that provides courses for a wide range of outdoor sports and activities. Details of the courses are found on the centre's website, part of which is shown below.

Rock Climbing

Rock Climbing is one of the most popular activities run by the centre. Click on the links below for more information.

(a) The web page on Rock Climbing includes a series of images as well as an audio voice-over. Some of the images have been *cropped*.

   (i) What happens to an image when it is cropped?

_____

_____

1
0

   (ii) State **one** method of *capturing images* for a web page.

_____

_____

1
0

   (iii) State **one** method of *capturing audio* for a web page.

_____

_____

1
0

Page two

1. **(continued)**

(*b*) Access to the Internet is provided by an Internet Service Provider (ISP).

State **two** facilities that the ISP may offer to Glencoe House.

1 _____

_____

2 _____

_____

(*c*) When potential clients contact Glencoe House, the response sometimes includes an *attachment* saved as a *standard file format*.

(i) What is an attachment?

_____

_____

(ii) Name **one** standard file format

_____

(iii) Describe **one** advantage of using standard file formats.

_____

_____

_____

[Turn over

2. When clients make a booking, Mirrah, the centre's secretary, enters their details in a database.

(a) Mirrah has poor eyesight. State **two** ways in which her computer's *HCI* could be customised to enable her to carry out this task effectively.

1 _____

_____

2 _____

_____

Part of the database design is shown below.

Field Name	Type	Size	Validation	Sample Record
Client Code	Number	4	>0 and <9999	1342
Surname	Text	20		Astley
Firstname	Text	20		Mike
Address	Text	30		34 Brampton Rd
Town	Text	20		Barnsley
Postcode	Text	8		YK3 7HJ
Sex	Text	6		Male
Date of Birth	Date	6		03/11/78
Course Name	Text	20		Orienteering

(b) A *validation* check is shown. Name the type of validation used.

_____

(c) Describe the difference between *validation* and *verification*.

_____

_____

_____

_____

KU	PS

2. **(continued)**

(d) The centre's database currently holds information concerning 15,000 clients.

Calculate how many **bytes** will be required to store **all** records. (Show your working.)

_____

_____

_____

(e) Mirrah wants to produce a paper copy of all females who have booked the mountain biking course.

  (i) Describe how this could be done.

_____

_____

_____

_____

  (ii) In this example, is Mirrah a *data subject, data controller* or *data user*?

_____

  (iii) Describe **two** rights that a data subject has with the *Data Protection Act*.

   1 _____

    _____

   2 _____

    _____

(f) Many databases make use of *computed fields*. What is a computed field?

_____

_____

[Turn over

Margin marks:
- (d): PS 2 1 0
- (e)(i): PS 4 3 2 1 0
- (e)(ii): PS 1 0
- (e)(iii): KU 2 1 0
- (f): KU 1 0

3. Derek Summers is a programmer.

(a) Derek's programs have to be translated into *machine code* before processing can take place. This can be done using either an *interpreter* or *compiler*.

Which type of translator would Derek use in the following situations? Explain why.

(i) While developing the program: _____

Reason _____

_____

_____

_____

2
1
0

(ii) When the program is finished: _____

Reason _____

_____

_____

_____

2
1
0

(b) Derek always tries to make sure his software is *portable*. Explain why he does this.

_____

_____

_____

1
0

3. **(continued)**

(*c*) Most of Derek's software is *commercial*. Some of it is *shareware*.

(i) What is shareware?

_____

_____

_____

(ii) Why do you think Derek distributes his work as shareware?

_____

_____

_____

(*d*) Some of Derek's customers download his software, while others receive their copies by post.

State **one** reason why Derek may prefer his customers to download his software.

_____

_____

_____

(*e*) All of Derek's software includes *on-line help* and *on-line tutorial* facilities.

Which of these facilities should new customers use when they first receive the software? State **one** reason for your answer.

Facility _____

Reason _____

_____

_____

[Turn over

4. Derek enjoys river kayaking in his spare time. He is keen to extend his skills and has enrolled on a course of sea kayaking at Glencoe House.

(a) A week before the course is due to begin, he receives a *standard letter* confirming his place on the course.

   (i) What is a standard letter?

_____

_____

_____

_____

   (ii) Apart from a word processor, what other application is usually involved in the creation of standard letters?

_____

   (iii) State the name of the process that inserts information from this application into the word processed document.

_____

(b) On arrival at the centre, Derek is given a *magnetic stripe card* to access his accommodation. To enter his room, he must pass the card through a special piece of hardware.

What is this hardware called?

_____

(c) Derek finds an *expert system* providing advice on activities, particularly useful.

Describe **two** advantages of using expert systems.

1 _____

_____

2 _____

_____

4. **(continued)**

(*d*) The centre has a *client-server* network.

(i) State **two** advantages for the centre of using a client-server network.

1 _____

_____

2 _____

_____

(ii) What piece of hardware will have to be installed in each computer to allow access to the client-server network?

_____

(*e*) The centre is considering installing a *wireless* network. State **one** disadvantage of a wireless network in this situation.

_____

_____

_____

(*f*) The manager of the centre used to travel to Glasgow to attend a meeting with other outdoor centre managers. They now use *video conferencing* instead.

(i) State **one** input device required to use video conferencing.

_____

(ii) State **one** advantage to the managers of using video conferencing instead of attending their monthly meeting.

_____

[Turn over

5. Before heading out on his first sea kayaking activity, Derek uses a *virtual reality simulation* to practise the techniques.

(*a*) Apart from practising new techniques, suggest **two** other reasons why simulators are used by learners.

1 _____

_____

2 _____

_____

(*b*) When he uses the kayak simulator, sensors on the paddle detect the direction of movement and force used. This information is processed and a large *TFT* monitor displays the results of Derek's efforts.

(i) What type of converter will be needed **before processing** of the information can take place? Tick (✓) **one** box only.

D to A converter ☐   A to D converter ☐

2
1
0

1
0

5. **(b) (continued)**

(ii) The program controlling the kayak is stored on *ROM*. State **two** advantages of storing software on ROM.

1 _____

_____

2 _____

_____

(iii) What does TFT stand for?

T _____ F _____ T _____

(iv) State **one** other example of an output device that could be used specifically in a virtual reality system.

_____

[Turn over

6. At the end of the course. Derek prepares to depart.

(a) During the activity, several black and white photographs were taken of Derek and the other clients. He wishes to take copies of them home using his *USB flash drive*.

(i) He has only 3 Mb of storage space left on his flash drive. Each photograph measures 800×800 pixels. How many photographs can be stored on his flash drive?
(Show all working.)

_____

_____

_____

_____

**3
2
1
0**

(ii) The *operating system* is involved in transferring the images from the computer to the flash drive. State **two** functions of an operating system.

_____

_____

_____

**2
1
0**

(b) Derek pays for his course by *Electronic Funds Transfer* (*EFT*) using his *smart card*.

(i) Describe **one** advantage of using a smart card.

_____

_____

**1
0**

(ii) What are the main stages involved in EFT?

_____

_____

_____

_____

**3
2
1
0**

7. The centre uses a spreadsheet to keep track of its clients' accounts. Part of the spreadsheet is shown below.

	A	B	C	D	E
1	Name	Total Cost	Discount	Amount Paid	Money Due
2	Dino Mancini	520	52	300	168
3	Isla Sutherland	800	80	700	20
4	Sparky Douglas	280	0	200	80
5	Jack Valman	350	0	350	0

(a) Cell C2 contains a *function* that determines any discount due to the client. If a client spends £500 or more on a course, then a discount of 10% is given, otherwise they receive no discount.

Part of the function is shown below. Complete the function.

= _____ (B2>=500, _____, 0)

(b) This function has been replicated from cell C2 into cells C3 to C5. What type of reference has been used?

Type of reference _____

Explain your answer _____

_____

_____

(c) At the end of each month, course directors receive a word processed report containing bar charts showing the number of clients completing their courses and the amount of money due. This information changes from month to month.

What type of linkage has taken place between the word processor and the spreadsheet applications?

Type of linkage _____

Explain your answer _____

_____

_____

[Turn over

Margin marks: 2 1 0 · 1 0 · 1 0 · 1 0 · 1 0

7. **(continued)**

(*d*) The client bookings database is a *multi-user* database. It is password protected in an attempt to prevent unauthorised access and hacking.

(i) What piece of legislation makes this activity an offence?

_____

(ii) What other activity is outlawed in this legislation?

_____

(iii) What type of access would be suitable in this situation – *random* or *sequential*?

Type of access _____

Explain your answer _____

_____

_____

[END OF QUESTION PAPER]

[BLANK PAGE]

G

KU   PS

Total Marks

0560/402

NATIONAL QUALIFICATIONS 2008

MONDAY, 12 MAY 10.20AM – 11.35AM

COMPUTING STUDIES STANDARD GRADE
General Level

Fill in these boxes and read what is printed below.

Full name of centre

Town

Forename(s)

Surname

Date of birth

Day Month Year   Scottish candidate number   Number of seat

Read each question carefully.

Attempt **all** questions.

Write your answers in the space provided on the question paper.

Write as neatly as possible.

Answer in sentences wherever possible.

Before leaving the examination room you must give this book to the invigilator. If you do not, you may lose all the marks for this paper.

1. Saunders High School are raising money for charity. Ben has entered the money raised from a "car washing" event in the spreadsheet below.

	A	B	C	D	E
1	**Car Washing**				
2					
3		**Feb**	**Mar**	**Apr**	**Best Month**
4	Andrew	£10.70	£3.50	7.1	£10.70
5	Arif	£2.00	£1.10	9	£9.00
6	Hassan	£7.10	£3.20	1.82	£7.10
7	Michael	£6.40	£8.30	2.3	£8.30
8	Christine	£5.80	£6.10	3	£6.10
9					
10				**Average**	**£8.24**

(a) The values in column D have to be formatted to look like those in columns B and C.

Describe how this can be done.

_____

_____

_____

_____

(b) In cells **E4** and **E10** functions have been used.
Complete the following.

(i) E4 =_____ (_____:_____)

(ii) E10 =_____ (_____:_____)

1. (continued)

(c) Cells E4 to E8 each contain a formula. This formula was only entered once in cell E4

    (i) Describe how this formula was *replicated*.

_____

_____

_____

_____

    (ii) Ben wants to stop people from changing his formulae. Explain what feature he must use to stop this happening.

_____

_____

(d) The headteacher would like to see the figures displayed as a bar chart but he is not familiar with the package. State the feature of the package that could help him.

_____

(e) The file is saved to a small portable device.

    (i) What is the name of this device?

_____

    (ii) State whether the file saved is an *application file* or a *data file*.

_____

    (iii) Explain the difference between an application file and a data file.

_____

_____

Margin marks: KU / PS columns — 2 1 0, 1 0, 1 0, 1 0, 1 0, 1 0

2. A library uses a database to hold the details of all of its books.

(*a*) A sample record is shown below.

Field Data	Sample Data	Field Type
Book Title	Treasure Island	Text
Cover	Treasure Island A Novel by Robert Louis Stevenson	**A**
Author	Robert Louis Stevenson	Text
ISBN	0448058251	**B**
Due to be returned	22/06/08	**C**
Keywords	Pirate, treasure, adventure, gold	Text

Identify the **field types** which are listed as A, B and C.

A = _____

B = _____

C = _____

(*b*) A *check digit* is used to ensure data is entered correctly.

(i) State the field in the record above that makes use of a check digit.

_____

(ii) Describe how a check digit is created.

_____

_____

_____

_____

2. (continued)

(*c*) Complete the following search screen to obtain a list of all adventure books written by Scott Miller due to be returned by 30/06/08.

LIBRARY DATABASE SEARCH SCREEN	
Book Title	
Author	
ISBN	
Due to be returned	Before 30/06/08
Keywords	
	SEARCH

(*d*) The librarian's computer is connected to a network which includes all of the libraries in the country.

What type of network is this?

_____

(*e*) State the term used to describe an attempt to gain illegal access to the library's network.

_____

[Turn over

3. The home page for a local builders' Web site is shown below.

**Aviemore	Torrance	Dennison**	
	This is the most popular design in our range of bungalows. Three bedroom, two bathroom, living room, dining room, kitchen, garage, GCH, DG.
	This is one of the smaller terraced houses. Three bedroom, two bathroom, living room, dining room, kitchen, garage, GCH, DG.
	This is a popular design in our detached house range. Three bedroom, two bathroom, living room, dining room, kitchen, garage, GCH, DG.

(a) When a user clicks on the word "Dennison", they are taken to a new Web page. State the name of this feature.

_____

(b) The image of the first house has been inserted incorrectly.

State **two** changes required to correct this problem.

_____

_____

_____

(c) The text for the web page was created in a *general purpose package*.

State the most suitable type of package for creating the text.

_____

1 0

2 1 0

1 0

3. **(continued)**

(d)   One of the paragraphs has been saved and inserted into the text for each house.

(i)   Name this type of paragraph.

_____

(ii)   State **two** advantages of using a pre-prepared piece of text.

1 _____

_____

2 _____

_____

(e)   A *high level language* was used to create the Web site.

(i)   Name a language that could be used to create Web pages.

_____

(ii)   State **two** common features of high level languages.

1 _____

2 _____

(iii)   What characters are used in *machine code*?

_____

(f)   The Web site includes many types of *multimedia*. State **one** type and explain how it could be used to improve the Web site.

Type: _____

Explanation:_____

_____

_____

_____

[Turn over

4. Morag uses *on-line banking* to check the balance of her account at ScotWide Bank.

(*a*)   Morag has a dial-up connection to the Internet.

(i)   State **two** disadvantages of using a dial-up connection.

1 _____

2 _____

(ii)   Name another type of connection.

_____

(*b*)   Morag cannot remember the Web address of the ScotWide Bank Web site. Using some of the words below, complete the sentences to describe how she can find her bank's Web site.

ScotWide   *engine*   *account*   *browser*

She would load up her _____ to view Web pages.

She would then use a search _____ and enter

_____ Bank.

(*c*)   Morag must enter two pieces of information to access her personal account. One of them is her username. State the other piece of information needed.

_____

(*d*)   What type of computer is used by the bank to store all of their customer details?

_____

4. (continued)

(e)   When Morag enters her details into her computer they are *encrypted* before being sent to the bank

    (i)   State what is meant by the term encrypted.

_____

_____

_____

    (ii)   Explain why her details have to be encrypted.

_____

_____

(f)   Morag's computer system has a LCD monitor. What do the initials LCD stand for?

L_____C_____ Display

[Turn over

1
0

1
0

2
1
0

5. CheapWays supermarket has installed a new checkout system.

(a) When an item is scanned, the price appears on the checkout display. What type of processing is this?

_____

(b) State **one** running cost of the new checkout system.

_____

(c) When a customer pays using a bank card, the money is taken from their account and transferred into the supermarket's bank account.

   (i) State the term used to describe this transfer of money.

_____

   (ii) State **one** advantage to the **supermarket** of this type of payment rather than paying with cash.

_____

_____

   (iii) State **one** advantage to the **customer** of this type of payment rather than paying by cash.

_____

_____

6. A factory currently employs people to make chairs. They are about to introduce an automated system.

(a) State **two** changes that may happen to the jobs of the workers.

1 _____

2 _____

(b) A person is employed to plan the new system.

(i) State the job title of this person.

_____

(ii) Name **two** other computing jobs, excluding the one used above, that might be needed in the factory.

1 _____

2 _____

(c) Use some of the words below to complete the paragraph about the new system.

tool   *mobile*   *feedback*

stationary   *sensor*   *robot*

When a chair moves along the conveyor belt it is detected by a

_____ which sends _____ to the main

computer. The conveyor belt stops and a robot uses a paint spraying

_____ to paint the chair. This type of robot is called a

_____ robot.

(d) State **two** ways that the robot could have been taught to paint the chairs.

1 _____

_____

2 _____

_____

[Turn over

7. Rebekkah is writing her life story using a word processing package. An extract is shown below.

Before my trip up the Amazon, I had to make sure that I had the following:

Checklist

Food	**Medical**	**Gear**
Beans	Bandages	Rope
Pasta	Plasters	Knife
Rice	Aspirin	Compass

(a) Rebekkah uses a spell checker to find mistakes in her document.

(i) Describe the steps that a spell checker takes when checking a word that is spelt incorrectly.

_____

_____

_____

_____

_____

(ii) The word Amazon is spelt correctly, but was identified as incorrect by the spell checker.

State how you could prevent "Amazon" from being highlighted by the spell checker.

_____

_____

7. (continued)

(b) Rebekkah notices that throughout her book she has called her friend "McGregor" instead of "MacGregor".

Describe how this could be corrected in a single operation.

_____

_____

_____

(c) Rebekkah wants to record images and sounds on her expedition.

State **two** input devices that she would need.

1 _____

2 _____

[*END OF QUESTION PAPER*]

[BLANK PAGE]

[BLANK PAGE]

C

KU   PS

Total Marks

0560/403

NATIONAL   MONDAY, 12 MAY
QUALIFICATIONS   1.00 PM – 2.45 PM
2008

COMPUTING STUDIES
STANDARD GRADE
Credit Level

Fill in these boxes and read what is printed below.

Full name of centre

Town

Forename(s)

Surname

Date of birth

Day   Month   Year   Scottish candidate number   Number of seat

Read each question carefully.

Attempt **all** questions.

Write your answers in the space provided on the question paper.

Write as neatly as possible.

Answer in sentences wherever possible.

Before leaving the examination room you must give this book to the invigilator. If you do not, you may lose all the marks for this paper.

1. Bethany owns the Blue Gables Hotel. She is trying to encourage more guests to stay at the hotel.

She sends out *standard letters* offering special deals to people who have stayed in the hotel before. The letters all contain the same information apart from the personal details such as name and address which will be inserted.

(a) Name the process that is described above.

_____

(b) Before printing the letters, Bethany uses both the *spell checker* and the *grammar checker*.

State an example of a mistake that would be picked up by each of these proofing tools.

Spell Checker _____

Grammar Checker _____

(c) Bethany designs a poster to advertise her hotel.

(i) State a suitable application package for her to use and explain your choice.

Suitable Package _____

Explanation _____

_____

1. (c) (continued)

(ii) She includes the logo from the Tourist Information Web site on her poster.

Explain why Bethany might be breaking the law by using this graphic.

_____

_____

_____

(iii) State how Bethany could include this logo from the Tourist Information Web site without breaking any laws.

_____

_____

(d) The logo she finally includes is represented in black and white. It contains 267200 pixels in total.

Calculate the storage requirement of this graphic in **kilobytes**. Show all your working.

_____

_____

_____

_____

(e) Bethany also includes one of her own photographs.

She wants to remove part of the picture as shown below.

State the most suitable tool for Bethany to use

_____

Part to be removed

[Turn over

Margin marks: 1 0 / 1 0 / 2 1 0 / 1 0

2. "Buzz" is a company which designs and manufactures digital alarm clocks.

Management is currently considering automating the entire process so they employ a *systems analyst*.

(a) Describe **two** tasks the systems analyst will perform.

1 _____

_____

_____

2 _____

_____

_____

(b) State **two** economic implications to the company if they go ahead with the systems analyst's recommendations.

1 _____

_____

_____

2 _____

_____

_____

(c) When factories are designed for robots they look very different from those designed for humans.

State **two** ways in which they differ.

1 _____

_____

_____

2 _____

_____

_____

2 1 0

2 1 0

2 1 0

2. **(continued)**

(*d*) The digital alarm clocks let you wake up to music playing from an audio CD. The clocks contain a *Digital* ⟶ *Analogue converter*.

Explain why the clocks must contain a Digital ⟶ Analogue converter.

_____

_____

_____

(*e*) A digital alarm clock is an example of an *embedded system*.

   (i) What is an embedded system?

     _____

     _____

   (ii) State the storage medium used by an embedded system.

     _____

[Turn over

3. Mohammad is a pupil at Alba Academy. He has broken his ankle and will have to work from home for the next month

His Computing teacher has asked him to research *mobile Internet technologies* and produce a report.

(*a*) State **two** mobile Internet technologies.

1 _____

2 _____

(*b*) He uses a *search engine* to help with his research.

What is a search engine?

_____

_____

_____

_____

(*c*) Mohammad becomes particularly interested in mobile Internet technologies that are manufactured in Japan.

(i) State a *complex* search that he could use in this situation.

_____

_____

_____

(ii) State **one** advantage of using a complex search rather than a simple search.

_____

_____

_____

KU	PS

3. **(continued)**

(d) He decides to word process his report and then *e-mail* it to his teacher as an *attachment*.

Mohammad realises that he should save his report using a *standard file format*.

   (i) State **two** suitable text formats that he could use.

   1 _____

   2 _____

   (ii) Explain why he should use a standard file format.

   _____

   _____

(e) As well as saving a copy of his report on the *hard disk*, he also saves it on his *USB flash drive*.

State **two** reasons why USB flash drives have become so popular.

1 _____

   _____

2 _____

   _____

(f) Mohammad could also have stored a copy of his report on a CD-RW.

What do the letters CD-RW stand for?

_____

_____

[Turn over

Margin marks: KU 210; PS 10; PS 210; KU 210

4. Rachel works in the administration department of her local college. She types up the students' projects and prints them out.

The college has recently bought a new printer for Rachel.

(a) State the piece of software necessary for the printer to work correctly.

_____

(b) The *operating system* on her computer has *background job capability*.

Explain why this could be an advantage to Rachel.

_____

_____

_____

_____

(c) One function of an operating system is *memory management*.

(i) State how each storage location in memory is identified.

_____

_____

(ii) Name the term used to describe the number of bits stored in each memory location.

_____

4. **(continued)**

(*d*) Another function carried out by an operating system is *file management*.

(i) State the type of filing system used to manage files shown in the diagram below.

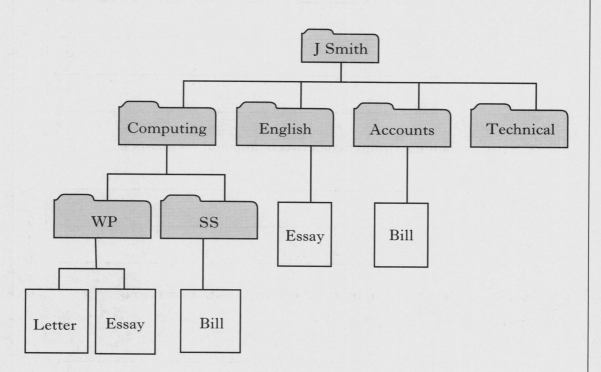

(ii) State **two** reasons for using this type of filing system.

1 _____

_____

2 _____

_____

[Turn over

5. At the headquarters of a well known bank, a *mainframe computer* system is used to process data.

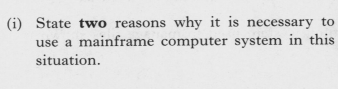

(*a*) (i) State **two** reasons why it is necessary to use a mainframe computer system in this situation.

1 _____

_____

2 _____

_____

(ii) Clearly explain the difference between *data* and *information*.

_____

_____

_____

(*b*) Most banks have started issuing their customers with *smart cards*.

State **two** reasons for doing this.

1 _____

_____

_____

2 _____

_____

_____

_____

2
1
0

2
1
0

2
1
0

5.   (continued)

(c) *Validation* and *verification* are two error checking processes.
Complete the table below.

Process	Meaning	Example
validation		Range Check
verification	Making sure that the data is entered correctly	

(d) (i) State **one** reason why banks are keen to promote *on-line banking*.

_____

_____

(ii) Do you think customers are happy with on-line banking?

☐ Yes   ☐ No   Tick (✔) **one** box.

Explain your answer making **two** clear points

_____

_____

_____

_____

(e) Computers make it easier to collect *management information*.

State **one** example of management information which would be useful to a bank manager.

_____

_____

_____

6. All the best young athletes in the country have been encouraged to attend a special training camp. They will each have three attempts to impress the coaches at their chosen event.

A target is set for each event. To represent their country, the athletes must achieve the target.

Below is part of a spreadsheet set up for the 100 metres sprint.

	A	B	C	D	E	F
1	**100 metres sprint**					
2						
3	**Under 16 Boys**			**Target Time (secs)**		**12.8**
4						
5	**Name**	**Race 1**	**Race 2**	**Race 3**	**Best Time**	**Represent Country?**
6	R Gracie	12.8	12.9	13.2	12.8	Yes
7	L MacAra	13.1	12.9	12.9	12.9	No
8	H Hunt	12.9	12.9	12.8	12.8	Yes
9	M Dykes	12.9	12.6	12.6	12.6	Yes
10	L Fraser	13.0	13.0	13.0	13.0	No

(a) State the formula that will be used to calculate R Gracie's best time in cell E6.

_____

(b) The formula in cell E6 is copied into cells E7 to E10.

(i) State the type of *referencing* used. Explain your answer.

Type _____

Explanation _____

_____

_____

_____

(ii) State another word for "copied" when referring to spreadsheets.

_____

2
1
0

2
1
0

1
0

KU | PS

6. (continued)

(*c*) State the type of formula contained in cell F6.

_____

1
0

(*d*) At the training camp, they are shown a multimedia presentation about the importance of keeping fit.

The presentation includes both *audio* and *video* elements.

State **two** ways that audio can be added to the presentation.

1 _____

_____

2 _____

_____

2
1
0

(*e*) The slides in this presentation are linked as shown below.

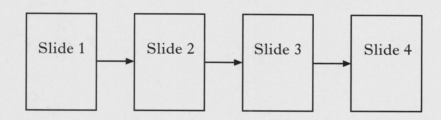

(i) State the type of linkage used above.

_____

1
0

(ii) Describe a way in which Slide 1 could directly link to Slide 3.

_____

_____

1
0

[Turn over

KU | PS

6.   (continued)

(f) At the end of the training camp all athletes are given a copy of the presentation on DVD.

Give **two** reasons why this would be a suitable storage medium.

1 _____

_____

2 _____

_____

(g) The athletes are told about an application package which would make decisions and offer advice about nutrition.

Name this type of package.

_____

7. A new medical centre has been opened in Bankness.

Computers are used to store the patients' data.

The computers are linked together to form a *Local Area Network* (LAN).

(a) The data held about patients is highly confidential.

   (i) Which Act states that data must be kept secure?

   _____

   (ii) State **one** other requirement of this Act when storing personal data.

   _____

   _____

(b) One way of keeping data secure is the use of *physical* methods.

   State **two** different physical methods.

   1 _____

   _____

   2 _____

   _____

(c) The network in the medical centre is one where many users can share the main computer's resources at the same time.

   (i) State the term used to describe this type of network.

   _____

   (ii) What piece of hardware is required on each of the stations to connect to the network?

   _____

[END OF QUESTION PAPER]

Margin marks: 10 ; 10 ; 210 ; 10 ; 10

[BLANK PAGE]

[BLANK PAGE]

[BLANK PAGE]

[BLANK PAGE]

[BLANK PAGE]

[BLANK PAGE]

[BLANK PAGE]